DOGS SET IV

Cavalier King Charles Spaniels

Cari Meister

ABDO Publishing Company

visit us at
www.abdopub.com

Published by ABDO Publishing Company, 4940 Viking Drive, Suite 622, Edina, Minnesota 55435. Copyright © 2001 by ABDO Consulting Group, Inc. International copyrights reserved in all countries. No part of this book may be reproduced in any form without written permission from the publisher.

Printed in the United States.

Cover Photo: Corbis
Interior Photos: Ron Kimball Studios (pages 5, 11, 19, 21), Corbis (pages 7, 15, 17), AP/Wideworld (pages 9, 13)

Editors: Bob Italia, Tamara L. Britton, Kate A. Furlong, Christine Fournier
Art Direction: Neil Klinepier

Library of Congress Cataloging-in-Publication Data

Meister, Cari.
   Cavalier King Charles spaniels / Cari Meister.
     p. cm. -- (Dogs, Set IV)
   Includes bibliographical references and index.
   ISBN 1-57765-475-7
    1. Cavalier King Charles spaniel--Juvenile literature. [1. Cavalier King Charles spaniel. 2. Dogs.] I. Title.

   SF429.C36 M45 2001
   636.752'4--dc21
   [B]

                                          00-045379

Contents

The Dog Family

All dog **breeds** belong to the Canidae **family**. Members of the Canidae family are called canids. Other canids include wolves, coyotes, jackals, and foxes.

Canids have similar **traits**. They have similar body shapes. They have an excellent sense of smell.

Long ago, dogs were wild animals like other canids. Later, people tamed dogs to help them with work, such as hunting and herding.

Eventually, dogs were trained to be good companions and friends. Today, there are more than 400 different dog breeds. One of the most popular is the Cavalier King Charles Spaniel.

The Cavalier King Charles Spaniel

Cavalier King Charles Spaniels

Cavalier King Charles Spaniels are **descendants** of dogs that have been around for hundreds of years. For centuries, toy spaniels were popular with England's **aristocracy**.

King Charles II had many toy spaniels. He was rarely without his little dogs. He **decreed** that the spaniels should be allowed in any public place, even **Parliament**!

Many years passed, and the toy spaniel's **characteristics** changed. In 1926, Roswell Eldridge offered a prize at Cruft's, England's most important dog show. Eldridge's prize was for dogs that resembled the toy spaniels from King Charles's time.

Many **breeders** worked to produce dogs that looked like King Charles's. In 1928, a dog named Ann's Son won the prize. All modern Cavalier King Charles Spaniels are **descendants** of Ann's Son. That same year, the name Cavalier King Charles Spaniel was chosen for the toy spaniels.

The Cavalier King Charles Spaniel has a long, majestic history.

What They're Like

Cavalier King Charles Spaniels are gentle, playful dogs. They like to sit on people's laps. Cavaliers do not need much exercise. Two or three short walks each day is enough.

Cavaliers are happy in both the city and the country. Though Cavaliers like the indoors, they love to explore outside, too. But Cavaliers should never be expected to run for very long. Cavaliers do not make good running partners.

Cavaliers were bred to be companion dogs. They look to their owners for leadership and guidance. As long as they spend most of the time with their owners, Cavaliers are happy dogs.

President and Mrs. Reagan with their Cavalier, Rex

Coat and Color

Cavalier King Charles Spaniels have long, silky, flowing coats. Their coats are straight, not curly.

If you want to enter your Cavalier in a dog show, do not cut its hair! In order for a Cavalier to win a prize, its hair must be natural.

Cavalier King Charles Spaniels come in four colors. They are Blenheim, tricolor, ruby, and black and tan.

Blenheim dogs have pearly white hair with large patches of chestnut color. Some dogs have a chestnut-colored mark on their foreheads. This is called the Blenheim spot. Dogs with this marking are rare and very desirable.

Tricolor dogs are pearly white with black and tan markings. Ruby dogs are a dark red color. Black and tan dogs are black with tan markings over their eyes, legs, chest, and tail.

This Cavalier puppy has a Blenheim coat.

Size

Cavalier King Charles Spaniels are small, limber dogs. They are usually between 12 and 13 inches (30-32 cm) tall. They weigh between 13 and 18 pounds (6-8 kg).

Cavaliers have large, round, dark brown eyes. Very few people can resist a Cavalier's facial expressions. Cavaliers are known for their sweet looks.

Cavalier King Charles Spaniels have long ears that are set high on their heads. When a Cavalier is alert, its ears come out a little bit around its face.

Most Cavalier King Charles Spaniels carry their tails in a happy, slightly wagging motion. Sometimes, their tails are docked, or cut short.

*The Cavalier's small size is ideal
for sitting on warm laps!*

Care

    Cavalier King Charles Spaniels are good companion dogs. They are loyal, happy, affectionate, and eager to please.

    It is important for owners to take good care of their Cavaliers. Like all dogs, Cavaliers need to visit a **veterinarian** once a year for a checkup. The veterinarian will give them shots to stop diseases like **rabies** and **distemper**.

    The veterinarian will also check the Cavalier's heart. Some Cavaliers have a heart problem called Mitral Valve Disease (MVD). MVD causes a valve in their heart to stop working properly. When you pick out your new Cavalier puppy, make sure it is checked for MVD.

Cavalier King Charles Spaniels need more attention than many other **breeds**. Cavaliers do not like to be alone. They like to be around people. They love hugs, kisses, and warm laps.

Cavaliers like to spend time with their owners.

Feeding

Like all dogs, Cavalier King Charles Spaniels need a meaty diet. Most dog foods you can buy at the store will give them the **nutrients** they need.

Some owners like to give their dogs bones. Cavaliers love to chew on bones. But do not give your Cavalier chicken, fish, pork, or lamb bones. These bones are brittle and break easily. If swallowed, the sharp ends could make holes in your Cavalier's stomach.

Cavalier King Charles Spaniel puppies need to eat several times a day. As the puppy grows older, it will need fewer meals. By the time the dog is two, one or two meals a day is best. Make sure that there is always fresh water available for your dog.

Puppies need to eat several times a day
so they can grow big and strong.

Things They Need

A Cavalier King Charles Spaniel needs to live indoors. It should not live outdoors. Cavaliers do poorly in very hot or very cold weather.

Cavalier King Charles Spaniels should have a quiet place to rest. An old blanket or dog bed in a quiet corner will do just fine.

Owners need to teach their dogs how to behave. When their dogs obey, owners should reward them with a treat or loving pat.

Like all dogs, Cavalier King Charles Spaniels need to wear dog tags at all times. The tag should have your dog's name, your name and address, and your telephone number. That way, if your dog gets lost, people will know who to call.

It is important that Cavaliers get plenty of rest.

Puppies

Mother Cavalier King Charles Spaniels will give many signals to let you know that her puppies are ready to be born. They will refuse to eat. They will be restless. They will want to go outside often.

Make sure there is a quiet place for the mother to have her puppies. A sturdy cardboard box lined with an old towel is a good place. Most Cavaliers have four or five puppies. Some have as many as nine puppies!

Cavalier King Charles Spaniels are tiny when they are born. They only weigh five to eight ounces (141-227 g).

Newborn Cavalier puppies cannot see or hear. But they have an excellent sense of smell. They use their sense of smell to find their mother. Until they are about three weeks old, the puppies get all the food they need from their mother's milk.

A Cavalier mother and her pups

Glossary

aristocracy: people who are born into a high social class. These people usually run the government.

breed: a group of dogs that share the same appearance and characteristics. A breeder is a person who raises dogs.

characteristic: a quality or feature that sets an individual or group apart from others.

decree: an official decision or order.

descendant: a dog born of a certain family or group.

distemper: a virus that dogs get. It causes breathing, stomach, and nerve problems.

family: a group that scientists use to classify similar plants and animals. It ranks above a genus and below an order.

nutrients: important parts of a diet that all living things need to survive.

Parliament: the highest lawmaking body of the English government.

rabies: a sickness of warm-blooded animals that causes abnormal behavior, increases saliva, and usually leads to death.

trait: the features of a person or animal.

veterinarian: a person with medical training who cares for animals.

Internet Sites

Cavalier King Charles Spaniel Club
http://www.ckcsc.org
The official Cavalier King Charles Spaniel Club site. Find out more about Cavaliers, locate breeders, and check out events in your hometown. This site even has a recipe for dog treats!

Cavalier Club of the United Kingdom
http://www.cavalierclub.co.uk
Read about the history of the Cavalier King Charles Spaniel and the standard of the breed. Learn about upcoming shows and events. Members' pages have great photos of award-winning Cavaliers.

American Cavalier King Charles Spaniel Club
http://www.ackcsc.org
The official site of the American King Charles Spaniel Club has information about Cavaliers and great photos of the different color types.

These sites are subject to change. Go to your favorite search engine and type in Cavalier King Charles Spaniels for more sites.

Index

A

Ann's Son 7

B

Blenheim spot 10
breeding 7, 8
build 12

C

Canidae 4
care 14, 18
Charles II, King of
    England 6
coat 10
color 10
Cruft's 6

D

dog show 6, 10

E

Eldridge, Roswell
    6
England 6
exercise 8

F

feeding 16, 20
food 16, 20

H

health 14, 16
history 4, 6, 7

M

Mitral Valve
    Disease (MVD)
    14

P

puppies 14, 16,
    20

S

size 12

T

temperament 8,
    12, 14, 15
training 18
traits 4

V

veterinarian 14

W

weight 12, 20